PERSPECTIVES ON EFFECTIVE TEACHING AND THE COOPERATIVE CLASSROOM

Judy Reinhartz, Editor

nea PROFESSIONAL LIBRARY
National Education Association
Washington, D.C.

Note

The opinions expressed in this publication should not be construed as representing the policy or position of the National Education Association. Materials published as part of the Analysis and Action Series are intended to be discussion documents for teachers who are concerned with specialized interests of the profession.

Acknowledgments

The following are used with permission from the sources indicated:

"Curriculum and Effective Teaching," adapted from "The School Program: Curriculum and Teaching in the 80's," by John I. Goodlad, pp. 71–77, *Education in the 80's: Curricular Challenges*. Copyright © 1981 by the National Education Association of the United States.

"The Art and Craft of Teaching," *Educational Leadership* 40, no. 4 (January 1983): 4–13. Reprinted with permission of the Association for Supervision and Curriculum Development. Copyright © 1983 by the Association for Supervision and Curriculum Development. All rights reserved.

"Overview of Cooperative Learning: A Strategy for Effective Teaching," adapted from the book *Our Classroom: We Can Learn Together* by Chick Moorman and Dee Dishon. © 1983 by Prentice-Hall, Inc. Published by Prentice-Hall, Inc., Englewood Cliffs, N.J. 07632. Reprinted with permission.

Library of Congress Cataloging in Publication Data
Main entry under title:

Perspectives on effective teaching and the cooperative classroom.

(Analysis and action series)
Includes bibliographies.
1. Teaching—Addresses, essays, lectures.   2. Motivation in education—Addresses, essays, lectures.
3. Education—Research—United States—Addresses, essays, lectures.   4. Education—United States—Addresses, essays, lectures.   I. Reinhartz, Judy.
II. Eisner, Elliot W.   III. Series.
LB1025.2.P413   1984   371.1'02   84–1176
ISBN 0-8106-1691-2

Contents

The Editor

Judy Reinhartz teaches at the University of Texas at Arlington. Dr. Reinhartz is the author of *Improving Middle School Instruction* (with Don M. Beach), published by NEA.

The Contributors

Arthur Costa, California State University, Sacramento

Dee Dishon, Institute for Personal Power, Portage, Michigan

Elliot W. Eisner, Stanford University, California

Robert Garmston, California State University, Sacramento

John I. Goodlad, University of California at Los Angeles

Philip L. Hosford, New Mexico State University, Las Cruces

Chick Moorman, Institute for Personal Power, Portage, Michigan

Pat Wilson O'Leary, Kalamazoo Valley Intermediate School District, Michigan

Georgea M. Sparks, Eastern Michigan University, Ypsilanti

Ralph W. Tyler, Director Emeritus, Center for Advanced Study of the Behavioral Sciences, Palo Alto, California

Introduction

The theme of this monograph is effective teaching and the cooperative classroom. The authors explore this theme in a variety of ways. Each chapter focuses on one or more aspects featured in the ten workshops that comprise the NEA in-service training program, *Effective Teaching and the Cooperative Classroom*.

In Chapter 1, "Research on Teacher Effectiveness: What It All Means," Sparks traces the research findings on effective teaching practices and educational outcomes during the last 15 years. She presents a rationale for the productive use of these practices as a means of improving American education. Taken together, the studies cited provide information based on successful teaching techniques. According to Sparks, most researchers caution against using the findings to judge teachers' competencies. The usefulness of the research lies in helping teachers to reflect on these findings as they relate to their own teaching practices. The data derived from research studies provide a "common language" that enables teachers to examine their teaching behavior and to put into practice those techniques found to be effective. The author also briefly summarizes the research on cooperative group learning strategies.

In Chapter 2, "Curriculum and Effective Teaching," Goodlad presents information from his study on schooling. Students in this study were asked, "What is the one best thing about this school?" Their responses were friends and sports activities; classes and teachers ranked third and fourth, respectively. Friends and sports activities are certainly an integral part of schooling, but equally important are classes and teachers. A prerequisite of effective teaching and the cooperative classroom is to study the teaching act and to link this study with effectively organizing the curriculum (classes) and what is known about students and learning. The implication of this goal should be at the top of our educational agenda.

For the goal of effective schooling to become a reality, as advocated by Goodlad, schools must become places in which teachers facilitate student learning. To do this in a cooperative classroom, teachers design an instructional program that encourages the development of individualities in all members of the school-age population by providing a varied curriculum menu and by involving students in a variety of learning activities.

The literature is replete with information that says effective schools have effective teachers. What does it mean to be an effective teacher?

Effective teachers understand the pedogogical principles and research associated with teaching and learning. The principles or "rules of thumb" as Eisner calls them in Chapter 3, "The Art and Craft of Teaching," guide teachers as they orchestrate the interaction of classroom life and activities. With the development of teacher skills, the movements within the instructional orchestration process create "an educationally productive tempo within a class." Flexibility helps teachers adapt to unexpected opportunities. A cooperative classroom encourages teachers to be creative and inventive when planning new teaching forms and moves. For Eisner, effective teachers are imaginative and are willing to continue to learn and grow beyond their existing teaching repertoire. By incorporating new skills into an existing repertoire, teachers form a productive, eclectic base for deciding the appropriate types of teaching "moves."

Teacher evaluation has numerous connotations. In Chapter 4, "These Days—These Debates," Hosford tackles this topic. He argues for the use of both a quantitative and a qualitative approach to gaining knowledge about teacher effectiveness. According to Hosford, "We [teachers] can get better; we [teachers] want to get better; and we [teachers] can improve—but only through calm, scholarly evaluations of our teaching for the purpose of self-improvement." He also suggests criteria for achieving schoolwide consensus regarding the process of performance evaluation of teachers.

In Chapter 5, "Aldo: A Metaphor," Garmston and Costa provide a short narrative about a teacher with 25 years of classroom experience. Aldo is concerned about the new move toward teacher accountability through evaluation, he is scared about complying with district policy, and he is unsure about what administrators expect of him—"he doesn't quite know if he's capable of doing that."

The case study provides a portrait of a teacher who cares very deeply for children and who provides them with generous amounts of individual attention. For the past 25 years, Aldo has been his own instructional person, but recently the district has adopted an aggressive staff development program called PRAISED. What do you think Aldo should do instructionally? What should administrators, including Aldo's principal, do to help Aldo grow professionally and personally?

Beneath the outlandish exterior of this scenario, the reader is led to believe there is such a teacher who is concerned and confused about his professional future. This open-ended situation raises the issue of staff development as it relates to effective teaching and individual teaching philosophy and style. School districts can benefit from developing in-service programs that provide a supportive, nurturing environment in which all teachers—especially the Aldos—can learn about and implement newly acquired teaching skills.

According to Tyler in Chapter 6, "Using Research to Improve

Teaching Effectiveness," developing and improving any profession "... depends upon the skill and dedication of its practitioners and the relevant knowledge available for their use." Unlike other professionals who readily use research information, educators are often confused about which data to use, or they perhaps are unaware that it is available.

Tyler challenges educators to use what is available from "action research," but reminds them that research findings are generalizations that serve to guide practitioners as they study and try to understand a particular school, classroom, student, teacher, or parent. Teachers are, then, responsible for identifying and analyzing their own situations and problems. Effective teachers should, therefore, use the research information as a frame of reference as they decide on tentative solutions to instructional problems, test these solutions, and verify or refute their interpretations.

While the foregoing chapters deal with the broader aspects of effective teaching and the cooperative classroom, the last chapter prepares teachers more directly for the implementation of these ideas in the classroom. In Chapter 7, "Overview of Cooperative Learning: A Strategy for Effective Teaching," Moorman, Dishon, and O'Leary give their rationale for teaching cooperation. They also describe the differences between typical classroom groups and cooperative groups, noting that traditional classrooms emphasize individualized and competitive goal structures. According to the authors, "cooperation is a way of behaving that doesn't just happen." Cooperative skills must be taught. Teachers can teach their students these skills and build interdependence by having students work in groups on a single product and then rewarding them on the basis of the group's work. By teaching cooperative behaviors teachers also can achieve a balance between the three types of goal structures—individualized, competitive, and cooperative. In this way they help their students acquire the variety of skills necessary for more effective learning not only in school but in later life and work.

Cooperative classrooms reflect the best of what is known about the teaching act and the learning process; teachers in these classrooms are effective and work from an awareness level that is founded upon a sound theoretical base. Effective teachers have been described as having a finite number of managerial, instructional, and organizational skills that differentiate them from ineffective teachers. It is the effective teachers who create a cooperative classroom climate that puts students in touch with the curriculum and who utilize strategies that continue to keep them in touch.

—*Judy Reinhartz*

Chapter 1

Research on Teacher Effectiveness: What It All Means

Georgea M. Sparks

Several national reports on educational excellence in 1983 and 1984 highlighted the importance of the quality of classroom instruction. Everyone is interested in improving the teaching and learning process in our schools. Yet, everyone seems to have a pet theory of how to improve instruction. The wide variety of programs, techniques, and curricula is mind boggling!

Fortunately, we have over 15 years of research on effective teaching practices to guide us in improving education. This research has highlighted several sets of teaching behaviors that are known to cause higher student achievement gains. Experimental studies have established that teachers can learn to use these practices and that student learning gains rise significantly as a result of these changes in practice.[8]

Clearly, this body of research has important implications for those who wish to improve American education. But the findings must be interpreted cautiously. This chapter describes the research methods in an effort to show how they can and cannot be applied to the realities of the classroom. Then it discusses the findings. Finally, it proposes a rationale for the productive use of the research.

RESEARCH ON TEACHER EFFECTIVENESS: METHODS AND ISSUES

In the early 1970's, several large-scale studies examined teaching styles and student outcomes. At first, these studies took the form of process-product correlational studies. Researchers described and measured what teachers did in their classrooms (process). Then they measured student gains on basic skills, usually reading and math (product). Next, they looked for relationships between the teaching practices and student achievement gains. This line of research yielded some impressive and consistent results: teachers who used certain teaching practices more often had higher class average learning gains. For example, in the primary grades, a clear system of classroom rules, small-group or whole-class teaching, and assuring high success on questions were associated with greater student reading and math gains.[6]

By the late 1970's, an impressive array of such practices had been compiled. But the correlational methods used did not allow any generalizations to be made concerning the causes of the learning gains. Nor had it been established that teachers could make changes in their teaching to more closely match the "effective" styles. The next step was to conduct experiments to train an experimental group of teachers to use the methods indicated by research to promote student achievement. A matched control group taught as usual. Observations were made to establish the extent to which the trained teachers used the recommended practices. Average achievement test gains of the two groups of students were then compared. In over five such experiments conducted throughout the country, students of the experimental-group teachers gained significantly more than did students of the control-group teachers.[8] Consequently, it could be said that when teachers used certain practices, student learning increased.

Before describing these findings, it is important to caution the reader about their interpretation and application. First, it must be remembered that the research methodology required the use of reliable and valid measurement instruments to observe teaching behaviors. Thus, any behavior that could not be clearly seen and measured was not included as a research variable. Clearly, there are many critically important aspects of the teaching act that are difficult to measure reliably and objectively. The fact that certain subtle teaching practices do not appear in the research findings is more a result of the method than an indication of their lack of importance.

Second, the product or outcomes studied were almost always standardized achievement test scores. Again, the fact that other important educational outcomes do not often appear in the research does not mean that such outcomes are not important; it simply means that they were not easily measured in these studies.

FINDINGS ON TEACHING EFFECTIVENESS

One of the earliest large-scale studies of teacher effectiveness was the Beginning Teacher Evaluation Study (BTES).[5] Students and teachers in second- and fifth-grade classes were observed throughout this multiyear study. Correlations with learning gains in reading and math yielded the concept of Academic Learning Time (ALT)—the time students spent engaged in relevant learning activities at a high success rate. The more ALT, the higher the learning gains. It was also found that teachers having the greatest gains used a systematic model of teaching that included diagnosis, prescription, presentation, monitoring, and feedback.

The alarmingly high variation among the BTES classrooms in the amount of engaged student time highlighted the importance of classroom management and the use of classroom time. Studies at both the elementary[3] and secondary levels[21] have illuminated several effective classroom management strategies. In general, teachers who, at the beginning of the year, spent considerable amounts of time "teaching" their students how to behave in their classrooms had the highest levels of student time on task (and thus achievement). Planning for the use of space, classroom routines, and class rules and consequences was an important activity for these "proactive" (as opposed to "reactive") classroom managers. These teachers gave clear directions, checked for understanding, and monitored carefully. They made sure students always had something useful to do. They kept things moving through brisk pacing of lessons, smooth transitions, and by offering a balanced diet of various types of activities.

Teacher expectations, or the "Pygmalion Effect,"[12] is another area highlighted by the classroom observation research. Good and Brophy[9] found that teachers tended to treat students they identified as "high achievers" and those they identified as "low achievers" in very different ways. In general, the low expectation students had fewer opportunities to participate and received lower quality feedback and less teacher attention. Clearly, such unwitting treatment of lower achieving students could result in a self-fulfilling prophecy, with lower achievers relegated to the slower groups and rarely rising from those levels. Fortunately, the researchers found that simply making teachers aware of these tendencies enabled them to avoid the inequities.

A final area of research on teacher effectiveness goes back to the BTES findings—how the teacher structures and conducts the instructional activities. The systematic behaviors of diagnosis, prescription, explanation, monitoring, and feedback have been extended by the work of Hunter"[11] and by advocates of Mastery Learning—for example, Bloom.[1] Rosenshine[15] has also described many of the effective instructional techniques in his reviews of the process-product research. In general, the practices recommended by these experts include having a clear objective, often derived from a task analysis; diagnosing learners to make sure instruction is targeted at the correct level of difficulty; providing an "anticipatory set," including focusing activities, an overview, and the objective and purpose of the lesson; providing information in small steps, with modeling and checking for understanding; guided practice with immediate feedback and high success rate; independent practice and/or reteaching; and review and closure. These strategies are not intended as a recipe, but rather, they are found in varying degrees in effective classrooms.

In addition to the preceding findings, another important area of research should be mentioned. Although the process-product methodology was not used in these studies, the findings are convincing and important for educators to consider. A group of studies has examined cooperative group learning strategies that combine students into heterogeneous teams (according to ethnicity and/or achievement level) to work together and to help one another learn. In some of the models, students have specific roles; in others, student groups compete against one another for prizes and privileges. In general, it has been documented that students benefit from such group structures by learning more and by cooperating more willingly with those from other cultural and/or ability groups.[16]

IMPLICATIONS FOR TEACHERS

What are the implications of the research on teacher effectiveness for teachers? Most researchers who have translated their work into training programs emphasize strongly that the findings are not to be used to judge teachers' competencies. Rather, they prefer to share the findings with teachers and ask them how they might be applied to their situations. Since no teacher's classroom is exactly like those used in the research studies, blind transfer of the findings to every educational setting would be a serious error (not to mention the risk of alienating many excellent teachers). The usefulness of the research, most would agree, is to help teachers reflect on their own practices in light of the findings. It is most helpful as a set of concepts (or a common language) that enables practitioners to analyze, reflect upon, and discuss the effects of their teaching behavior on student learning.

Many critics of effective teaching research have objected to the fact that often it is referred to as a panacea—"If only all our teachers get trained in this or that program, then all will be fine." Unfortunately, this is not the case. Many valid and important aspects of teaching and learning are not addressed by the research, mainly because of the methodological limitations mentioned. The majority of the research has focused on those teaching behaviors and student learnings that can be measured and quantified.

No one with teaching experience (and virtually all the researchers cited here have been teachers) would suggest that all lessons be taught through direct instruction or mastery learning approaches. The interpreters of this research need to recognize the importance of using various methods to teach the higher-level skills of categorizing, analyzing, hypothesizing, generalizing, predicting, and justifying, among others. It seems that the most effective teachers (in the affective domain and in the entire range of the cognitive domain) use a variety of techniques, many

11

of which are included in the research. Surely, for skills commonly tested by achievement tests, it makes sense to use the practices that research indicates are most effective; but for many valuable educational outcomes, other models or techniques come into play.

Finally, it should be mentioned that researchers are energetically pursuing a deeper understanding of how higher-level thinking skills are best taught. It may be several years before their findings become available and applicable to classrooms. Still, the quest goes on.

REFERENCES

[1]Bloom, B. S. *Human Characteristics and School Learning.* New York: McGraw-Hill, 1976.

[2]Emmer, E.; Evertson, C.; Sanford, J.; Clements, B.; and Worsham, M. *Classroom Management for Secondary Teachers.* Englewood Cliffs, N.J.: Prentice-Hall, 1984.

[3]Evertson, C.; Emmer, E.; Sanford, J.; and Clements, B. "Improving Classroom Management: An Experiment in Elementary Classrooms." *Elementary School Journal,* January 1984.

[4]_____. *Classroom Management for Elementary Teachers.* Englewood Cliffs, N.J.: Prentice-Hall, 1984.

[5]Fisher, C.; Marliave, R.; and Filby, N. "Improving Teaching by Increasing 'Academic Learning Time'." *Educational Leadership* 37, no. 1 (October 1979).

[6]Gage, N. L. *The Scientific Basis of the Art of Teaching.* New York: Teachers College Press, 1978.

[7]_____, and Berliner, D. C. *Educational Psychology.* 3d ed. New York:. Longman, 1984.

[8]_____, and Giaconia, R. "Teaching Practices and Student Achievement: Causal Connections." *New York University Education Quarterly,* May 1981.

[9]Good, T., and Brophy, J. *Looking in Classrooms.* New York: Harper and Row, 1978.

[10]Good, T., and Grouws, D. "The Missouri Mathematics Effectiveness Project: An Experimental Study in Fourth-Grade Classrooms." *Journal of Educational Psychology* 71, 1979.

[11]Hunter, M. *Rx Improved Instruction.* El Segundo, Calif.: T.I.P. Publications, 1976.

[12]Jacobson, L., and Rosenthal, R. *Pygmalion in the Classroom: Teacher Expectation and Pupils' Intellectual Development.* New York: Holt, Rinehart, and Winston, 1968.

[13]Joyce, B. and Weil, M. *Models of Teaching.* Englewood Cliffs, N.J: Prentice-Hall, 1972.

[14]Kerman, S. "Teacher Expectations and Student Achievement." *Phi Delta Kappan,* June 1979.

[15]Rosenshine, B. "Teaching Functions and Instructional Programs." *Elementary School Journal* 83, no. 4, 1983.

[16]Slavin, R. "Cooperative Learning." *Review of Educational Research* 50, 1980.

[17]_____. *Cooperative Learning: Student Teams.* Washington, D.C.: National Education Association, 1982.

[18]_____. *Student Team Learning: An Overview and Practical Guide.* Washington, D.C.: National Education Association, 1983.

[19]Sparks, G. M., and Sparks, D. C. *Effective Teaching for Higher Achievement.* Videotapes available from ASCD, 225 N. Washington St., Alexandria, Va. 22314.

[20]Stallings, J., and Kaskowitz, D. *Follow Through Classroom Observation Evaluation, 1972-1973.* Menlo Park, Calif. Stanford Research Institute, 1974.

[21]Stallings, J.; Needels, M.; and Stayrook, N. *How to Change the Process of Teaching Basic Reading Skills in Secondary Schools: Phase II and Phase III Final Report.* Menlo Park, Calif.: Stanford Research Institute, 1978.

Chapter 2

Curriculum and Effective Teaching

John I. Goodlad

> The facts of our twentieth century life—a rapidly changing society, a mounting store of knowledge, and new understandings about people and about learning—create some basic problems relating to the instructional program of the schools. There is no shortage of ideas about what these problems are and how they should be solved. There is, in fact, a constant babble of voices as millions of people with many and often conflicting ideas speak out about education.[1]

The broad facts of twentieth century life remain, intensifying old problems and creating new ones. The babble of voices continues. And the need to find a guiding sense of direction for the schools is as great as or greater than it was two decades ago.

Several of the questions posed today about education invite the development of a curriculum agenda for the 80's. One question in particular guides what follows: How can the instructional program of the schools be designed to develop the individual potentialities of all members of the school population within the framework of a society that values both unity and diversity? Unfortunately, this question has not been well attended to. It has not been the subject of sustained dialogue at any level of the educational system—and our schools now show the signs of curricular neglect.

OLD PROBLEMS IN NEW DRESS

If preliminary findings from a small sample of carefully selected schools in "A Study of Schooling"[2] are at all representative of more schools, then momentous curriculum development tasks beg for attention. I use here, first, a cluster of data pertaining to the 13 senior high schools in our sample and, later, data from the 25 elementary and junior high schools—schools diverse in size, socioeconomic status and ethnicity of students, rural/metropolitan location, and regional distribution.

Our data suggest the dominance in these schools of two provisions for diversity. First, there appears to be an assumption that the school should assure, on the one hand, the preparation of students for more advanced studies and the professions and, on the other, the preparation to go into jobs before or directly after high school graduation. Clearly, there were students emphasizing academic subjects and there were students enrolled heavily in vocational courses. Often, the two types were quite out of balance in a student's curriculum. Counsellors and vocational education teachers in the high schools I visited told me that it would be very difficult—indeed, virtually impossible—for students emphasizing vocational studies to shift into an academic concentration and graduate in the normal time. In effect, there is in most of the high schools in our sample an academic track and a vocational track.

The second provision for diversity is found within the academic offerings. Eight of the thirteen schools were tracked in the four subject fields usually required for college admission (mathematics, social studies, science, and English); the remaining five schools were tracked in three of these subjects. A major assumption underlying tracking has been the need to separate slower and faster students into different *levels* of the subject matter so that the bright students would not be slowed by the less able. (Although this assumption has been brought into question by research, it tends to persist.) But, in our sample of schools, this assumption has been expanded far beyond its traditional meaning. Commonly, we found students to be tracked not only into different levels of the same subjects but also into different subject matter. That is, those in the lowest tracks frequently were engaged in subject matter not previously encountered by students now in the upper tracks. Conversely, those in the upper tracks frequently were studying subject matter to which those in the lower tracks would not be exposed at some later time. Tracking, then, was not just in *level* but in *kind* of subject matter.

Ironically, in the name of individual variation, these schools may be giving up on individuals too soon, tracking them into self-fulfilling prophecies of low-paying jobs. Needless to say, many individuals so tracked will live lives that defy such prophecies, but they often will do so in spite of rather than because of their education in schools.

Most of us who pushed vigorously during the 60's and 70's for individualized learning had in mind the need to address the wide range of student attainment in any class of "graded" students—a range spanning about four grade levels at the fourth grade and increasing steadily with upward progression through the school. A major task for curriculum developers, we reasoned, was the identification of fundamental elements (concepts, principles, skills, values, and the like) to be learned by all students *commonly* but at different rates of speed. It would be necessary, we thought, to employ a variety of teaching techniques and, perhaps, even to differentiate for students of varying abilities the topics used for the ultimate mastery of these subject matter elements. But few of us had in mind accounting for human variability by separating students into differing streams of knowledge. This certainly is not what Bloom[3] envisions in his proposals for mastery learning.

What we hoped for was to link the growing understanding of people and learning with subject matter in organizing curriculums and in teaching. This goal remains elusive; its implications should be at the top of our educational agenda.

Again, data from "A Study of Schooling" illuminate the problem. From questionnaires filled out by students and from extensive classroom observations, it becomes apparent that the range of pedagogical procedures employed, particularly in the academic subjects, is very narrow. As in most classrooms observed in our earlier report *Behind the Classroom Door,*[4] the teaching observed in our current study was characteristically telling or questioning students, reading textbooks, completing workbooks and worksheets, and giving quizzes. This pattern became increasingly dominant with the progression upward from primary to secondary classes. Sadly, there were few signs to suggest increased efforts to reach slow learners in the lower tracks through more creative, nurturing pedagogy. Indeed, such evidence as there was to suggest imaginative teaching turned up somewhat more frequently in upper or advanced subject matter tracks.

If students are to learn, they must become engaged with the subject matter, whether it is a mathematical problem, the characteristics of some other culture, the shaping of clay, or the structure of a poem. This engagement does not occur similarly for all kinds of learning; nor does it occur similarly for all individuals, whatever the subject matter. A concept needs to be read about, talked about, written about, perhaps danced or acted out, and eventually used in some meaningful context.

But the forms of enticing the necessary engagement appeared to be limited in the classrooms of our sample, to become established by the upper elementary years, and to become rigid with upward progression. Of course, there were exceptions. Some teachers deviated from the pattern. But even in the arts, a considerable portion of the teaching was characterized by the kinds of activities described earlier as dominating the academic subjects. And although the teachers in our sample subscribed overwhelmingly to the importance of praise and encouragement in the learning process, we found little of it in the classroom. Further, the incidence of such teacher support declined steadily from the primary grades upward.

In responding to the question "What is the one best thing about this school?" the most frequently chosen answers at both junior and senior high levels were "my friends" and "sports activities." The "classes I'm taking" and "teachers" were relatively infrequently chosen categories. When asked who were the most popular students, "athletes" and "good looking kids" accounted for 60 percent of the junior high choices and a whopping 78 percent of the senior high choices. "Smart students" accounted for about 14 percent of the choices at the junior high level and only 7 percent at the senior high level. They apparently fare better in the peer group environment if they are also good looking athletes.

It would appear that our secondary schools are faced with a momentous challenge in seeking to engage the young in academic, intellectual pursuits. Large segments of our data suggest not only a declining engagement from primary to secondary grades but also a decline, or at least a leveling off, in pedagogical approaches designed to increase the appeal of academic learning. And another part of our data reveals a steady decline in students' academic self-concepts (e.g., feeling good about their schoolwork) with upward progression through school.

As a nation, we have been markedly successful in getting into schools a large percentage of school-age children and youth. But unless we are markedly more successful in involving young people in the learning activities that schools presumably should provide, we can expect this percentage to decline. The question arises as to whether we can make universal schooling work—especially if we believe that universal schooling means not only schools commonly attended but also things commonly learned.

TOWARD COMMON LEARNINGS, UNCOMMONLY TAUGHT

The challenge is to design instructional programs that develop the individual potentialities of all members of the school-age population. For me, one implication to be drawn from "A Study of Schooling" data is that the schools in our sample recognize diversity by providing a varied curricular menu but a relatively unvaried pedagogy. I would argue for the reverse: a relatively common curricular fare but maximally varied teaching methods.

Students from diverse backgrounds should be enrolled together in common learnings taught through ways deliberately designed to recognize and appeal to their individual learning styles and abilities. In addition, part of each student's program should be uncommon, designed to develop some unique talent or capability and to use all the educational resources of the community. The ratio of learnings engaged in commonly to those studied uncommonly might well be about nine to one in the primary years and decline steadily to about seven to three in the senior high school years.

Our concern for individuals as persons must push us away from giving up on their potential and depriving them of options by tracking them early into self-fulfilling prophecies involving limited expectations. Our concern for individuals as citizens and for a democratic society's need for educated citizens must push us away from segregated tracks for different "classes" of learners. The work of the common school—a school commonly attended, with things commonly studied but uncommonly

17

taught—is not finished. Indeed, our schools have been through a bulge in the enrollment of diversity. The challenge now is to educate this varied student population commonly.

The challenge comes after what has been a depressing decade for educators and schools. The back-to-basics movement has spoken to diminished curricular expectations and the lowest common denominators in teaching, not to comprehensive educational programs for all and innovations in teaching.

As we move through the 80's, however, there are some encouraging signs. More and more thoughtful people are coming to realize that mechanistic, rote teaching encourages mechanistic learning and not problem-solving ability and other complex, cognitive processes. Data from "A Study of Schooling" show that the parents studied in the sample want a full range of intellectual, social, vocational, and personal educational goals for their children. This should not surprise us. One is forced to wonder why we did not assess parental wishes more carefully before embarking on a course of diminished expectations.

The tasks of curriculum conceptualization and development are awesome. What constitutes a K–12 program designed to develop, in balanced fashion, the intellectual, social, vocational, and personal abilities of all children and youth? What organizational arrangements are most likely to assure sequential progress through such a program? What help and support must teachers receive if they are to be highly successful in engaging diverse groups of students in common learnings? What are the prospects for mobilizing community resources to provide the instruction and the role models needed for the development of unique, individual talents? And how can federal and state agencies be truly helpful to local schools in assuring high-quality delivery systems?

Most of these questions were neglected in the 70's. They now provide the curricular and instructional agenda for the 80's. Let us not allow lesser questions to push these aside.

REFERENCES

[1]Sand, Ole, in the preface to: Fraser, Dorothy M. *Deciding What to Teach;* Goodlad, John I. *Planning and Organizing for Teaching;* and Miller, Richard I. *Education in a Changing Society.* Washington, D.C.: National Education Association, 1963. (All volumes in the series were produced by the Project on the Instructional Program of the Public Schools.)

[2]For further information on the Study and the sample, see: Goodlad, John I.; Sirotnik, Kenneth S.; and Overman, Bette C. "An Overview of 'A Study of Schooling'." *Phi Delta Kappan* 61: 174–178; November 1979.

[3]Bloom, Benjamin S. *All Our Children Learning.* New York: McGraw-Hill Book Company, 1980.

[4]Goodlad, John I.; Klein, M. Frances; and others. *Behind the Classroom Door.* Worthington, Ohio: Charles A. Jones, 1970.

Chapter 3

The Art and Craft of Teaching

Elliot W. Eisner

My aim in this essay is to recover on a theoretical level what I believe practitioners—teachers and school administrators—have never relinquished in the private, quiet moments of their professional lives. I wish to help re-establish, to legitimatize, to publicly acknowledge the art and craft of teaching. To write about the art and craft of teaching in a period in which we are sending a space shuttle through the heavens, when we are able to place man on the moon and, as Frank Buck used to say, "to bring 'em back alive" is seemingly to hearken back to a bygone era. We pride ourselves, and we should, on the achievements of science and the technology science has made possible.

Indeed, to write about the craft of teaching today is likely to evoke images of the elderly working painstakingly on a handcrafted item in a tiny cottage located in a small village sitting next to the delicate but limited glow of a flickering fire. Our images of science and technology are much sleeker, and these images have penetrated contemporary education. In education we talk about diagnosis and prescription, of entry and exit skills, of the use of token economies, and of feedback loops for inputs that fail to meet specifications when they become output. Such talk reminds me of the story of a conversation between the senior officer of a large corporation and a new business school graduate:

> "Sir, I think that by bringing up a small model to simulate aggregate income-expenditure alternatives over various time frames, by integrating those results with appropriate ZBB reviews to assess minimum core expenditure levels, and then by relating to managers in an MBO framework, we can get this administration moving again," said the young colleague with eagerness and authority.

> The senior man gazed out the window, pondered the words so redolent with modern techniques, then spoke:

> "Shut up," he explained.[1]

Why is it the art and craft of teaching—and of school administration—should seem so quaint? Why is it that the art of teaching should be regarded as a poetic metaphor, but like poetry, more suited to satisfy the soul than to inform the head? Why is it that one so seldom hears of workshops or conferences devoted to the art and craft of teaching? And what would re-emergence of such concepts mean for the improvement of teaching and for educational administrators? To find out we must first look back in time.

When one examines the intellectual history of American education, particularly as it emerged during the 19th century, one finds that a distinctive form of professional preparation developed with the creation of the first state normal school in 1839.[2] By the end of the 1870s, 80 such schools had been established and by 1900 there were over 150.[3] When schools are established for training practitioners, it's nice to have something to teach them. During the same period in Europe and later in America the field of psychology was itself being formalized, and the work of Wilhelm Wundt in Germany, Francis Galton in England, and G. Stanley Hall and William James in the United States provided much of the substance on which to build a profession of education.[4] Hall, the first person to receive a Ph.D. in psychology from Harvard University in 1878,[5] was the father of the child study movement[6] and editor of the influential *Pedagogical Seminary*.[7] James, whose *Talks to Teachers*[8] remains a classic, was himself influenced by Wundt and later was to train the giant of American psychology, the man to whom B. F. Skinner once wrote: "I seem to identify your point of view with the modern psychological view taken as a whole. It has always been obvious that I was merely carrying on your puzzle box experiments. . . ."[9] That man was Edward L. Thorndike.

Thorndike was a great psychologist. He did about everything. He studied children's drawings, he studied handwriting, he studied aptitude and motivation, he wrote yards of books and articles, but what he did most was study learning. It was Thorndike who developed the idea of the S-R bond and who coined the term "Connectionism"[10]: Learning, he argued, was the result of connections in the cortex, connections strengthened by reinforcements provided to responses to particular stimuli. To the extent to which each stimulus was unique, the responses to be learned were also unique. Rationality was a concept fit for philosophy of mind, but not for a scientific psychology of learning.

As for the transfer of learning, Thorndike believed it was quite limited: One was able to transfer what one had learned only insofar as the elements in one situation were identical with those in the next. It was, as he called it, a theory of identical elements.[11] Memory drums, rat mazes, positive and negative reinforcement, frequency, recency, and intensity were the metaphors with which he worked. Thorndike's task was to develop a science of learning so that brick by brick a science of education could be built. For those seeking a respectable basis for teacher training and school administration, such a view was understandably attractive.

When the first issue of the *Journal of Educational Psychology* was published in 1910, it was Edward L. Thorndike who had the lead article. He wrote:

> A complete science of psychology would tell every fact about everyone's intellect and character and behavior, would tell the cause of every change in human nature, would tell the result which every educational force—every act of every person that changed any other or the agent himself—would have. It would aid us to use human beings for the world's welfare with the same surety of the result that we now have when we use falling bodies or chemical elements. In proportion we get such a science we shall become masters of heat and light. Progress toward such a science is being made.[12]

What we see here is a noble ambition, an expression of faith in the power of scientific inquiry to shape, indeed to determine the future, and thus to enable humankind to create a better, more predictable world. Science is, after all, associated with progress. To have a science of education is to have know-how, to understand not only what works, but why. A scientific technology of teaching would reduce noise in the system, make the system more systematic, more efficient, and hence give taxpayers the products they wanted schools to produce.

Science became the faith: scientific technology, the good works that the faith made possible.

It is hard to underestimate Thorndike's legacy. His ideas, his research, but even more his faith in science, helped set the tone for educational research for the next 70 years. To understand that tone is to understand why it is that the art and craft of teaching were and are regarded as relics having only marginal relevance to the study and practice of education.

But even as influential as Thorndike was, he was not alone in shaping assumptions on which current conceptions of teaching and education rest. During the same period the concept of scientific management, developed by Francis Taylor and applied to the problems of making industrial plants more efficient, also entered the educational scene.[13]

School administrators embraced scientific management as a way to reduce their vulnerability to public criticism and to make schools more efficient. In this approach management of education was hyper-rationalized. Teachers were regarded as workers to be supervised by specialists who made sure that goals were being attained, that teachers were performing as prescribed, and that the public who paid for the schools were getting their money's worth.

The guiding metaphor was industrial and the scope for personal ingenuity on the teacher's part was accordingly diminished.[14] The task was to get teachers to follow the one best method, a method that scientific management of education would prescribe. Thorndike's ideas, working in conceptual tandem with Taylor's, set a tone for American education that is still with us.

There are several characteristics of scientifically oriented ideology in education that deserve more than a casual mention. I say ideology because any perspective one embraces comes replete with values and assumptions about what is valid and trustworthy, what methods are legitimate, what counts as evidence, and hence helps determine the ends that are worth pursuing. If an aim cannot be accommodated within the dominant ideology, it is dropped from view; it is not considered meaningful.[15]

One assumption used in the effort to build a science of educational practice is that education cannot in principle become a discipline in its own right. It is rather "an area of study" and the most promising way to study that area is through the social science disciplines. The ramifications of this view were then and are today substantial. Consider only one—its impact on theory.

Since the concepts and categories that constitute theory in the social sciences were originally designed for noneducationally specific phenomena—rat maze learning, socialization in prisons, churches, and the home, for example—what such categories and theories illuminate is largely what education has in common with other phenomena rather than what is unique or special about schools, classrooms, teaching, or curriculum. The theoretical windows through which we peer circumscribe that portion of the landscape we shall see.

A second widely accepted assumption is that what we can learn through research about learning will be less ambiguous if the units treated are segmented and small. The operating belief is that once these small units are brought under control, variables can be isolated, effective educational treatments identified and then, finally, aggregated in order to build a technology of educational practice. First you learn how to introduce a lesson, then how to pose questions to students, then how to demonstrate a principle, then how to bring a lesson to closure, and when these and several other dozen—dare I say hundreds?—of teaching skills are learned, the ability to teach skillfully will have been achieved.[16]

Because long periods of experimental treatment time tend to lead to confounding—that is, long experimental periods increase the probability that uncontrolled variability will contaminate the treatment making the results difficult to explain—experiments in classrooms tend to be "cleaner" if they are brief.[17] The result is that much educational experimentation takes the form of commando raids designed to get in and out of classrooms in as little time as possible or consists of very short microexperiments that compare the effects of bits and pieces. The modal amount of experimental treatment time in experimental studies reported in the *American Educational Research Journal* in 1977–78 was about 45 minutes. Studies are undertaken that are designed to determine if giving an example first and then an explanation, or an explanation first and then an example make any difference. The tacit assumption is that such knowledge, although discrete, is cumulative and independent of context. The variations that are possible in such approaches are, of course, endless. Like tadpoles they come forth filling the pages of learned journals.

Third, because the believability of conclusions can be no greater than the reliability of the instruments used, instruments used to measure classroom practice and student learning need to be very reliable indeed. What this has meant all too often is that what is educationally significant but difficult to measure or observe is replaced with what is insignificant but comparatively easy to measure or observe.

Hence, we have a spate of studies that use the majestic to treat the trivial and others whose results are so qualified in character, for example, "The results hold for classrooms when the children are of low socioeconomic status if grouped homogeneously by reading score and taught by a male teacher who participated in at least five sessions of inservice education," that their practical utility is next to nil.

Fourth, and finally—although this critique could be extended further—is the assumption, and the primary one as far as I am concerned, that (1) a prescriptive educational science will make prediction and control of human behavior possible, and (2) such achievements are educationally desirable: the more prediction and control, the better. Prediction and control are of course virtues in the space program. The last place we want surprises is on the launching pad or on the moon. The best thing that can be said for such operations is that they were uneventful. But are such aspirations quintessential in education? Do we want—even if we could achieve it—to be able to predict and control all or even most of what a student will think, feel, or be? Is E. L. Thorndike's aspiration an appropriate one for education? Is Francis Taylor's model of scientific management what students need today? By this time you might have guessed that I have my doubts.

The critique I have provided concerning the aspiration to develop a science of education and the assumptions and consequences of that approach should not lead you to believe that I see no place for scientific study in education or that I believe that scientific metaphors should be replaced with artistic ones. This is not the case. What I do not believe holds promise in education is a prescriptive view of science. I do not believe that with greater specificity or by reducing the whole to its most essential parts we can produce the kind of prescriptions that have made the space shuttle, radar, or laser beam possible. The aspiration to create a prescriptive science of educational practice is, I believe, hopeless.

What I think scientific inquiry *can* provide in education are rules of thumb, not rules.[18] Rules of thumb are schematics that make interpretation and judgment more acute. Scientific inquiry can provide frames of reference that can sophisticate our perceptions, not mechanisms that will control the behavior of students, teachers, or administrators. In short, if a distinction can be made between the *prescriptive* and the *interpretive*, between rules and schematics, between algorithms and heuristics, in the human situation I opt for interpretation, schematics, and heuristics, rather than prescriptions, rules, and algorithms.

To assert these views is not to provide for holding them. Let me provide a few. First, those of us who work with human beings work with people who do not, despite Thorndike's view, simply respond to stimuli. Human beings *construe* situations, they make sense of classrooms, they anticipate the world in which they live. What constitutes a stimulus depends not simply on what is injected in the classroom but what students take from it. And what various students take from the classroom and what they make of what they take differs. It differs because of their prior experience, their capabilities, their friends, their predispositions, and their relationship with the teacher. Because the perspectives they bring are multiple, no teacher can depend on a script or a prestructured sequence for guarantees about effective teaching. Indeed, the more opportunities a teacher provides to students to idiosyncratically construe and express what they have gotten out of a lesson, the less the teacher controls what they are likely to learn: the students teach each other.

Second, what students learn from educational encounters increases the differences among them.[19] Students with high levels of interest and aptitudes for particular subjects are likely to go farther and faster. Their satisfactions are likely to be greater than their opposite. Students who are ingenious arrive at answers that are often unpredictable. Where in all of this is the power of a prescribed method of instruction? Unlike automobiles rolling down an assembly line where an additive model works fairly well (interaction effects are small), the children a classroom teacher deals with are unique configurations that change over time. Unlike electrons or billiard balls, students have ambitions and purposes and refuse to be treated as lumps of clay or sheets of steel passively awaiting the impact of a scientifically based teaching technology that provides little or no scope in its assumptions for what the students make of all of this. Our roles as teachers are closer to those of negotiators than to puppeteers or engineers. And even when we succeed in shaping our students' surfaces, unless we touch their souls we will be locked out of their inner lives. Much of contemporary education in both the public school and the university seldom gets more than skin deep.

Third, the idea that the skills of teaching can be treated as discrete elements and then aggregated to form a whole reflects a fundamental misconception of what it means to be skilled in teaching. What skilled teaching requires is the ability to recognize dynamic patterns, to grasp their meaning, and the ingenuity to invent ways to respond to them. It requires the ability to both lose oneself in the act and at the same time maintain a subsidiary awareness of what one is doing. Simply possessing a set of discrete skills ensures nothing.

The importance of perceiving patterns in motion while at the same time being able to monitor oneself should not come as a surprise to anyone who has reflected on what being in a social situation requires. Humans have a built-in need to seek structures of signification. They find it necessary to make sense of the world. They learn to improvise within a changing field, whether in the classroom, the board room, or the principal's office. The mechanical application of prescribed routines is the surest way I know of to get into trouble.

But what of the art and craft of teaching? Thus far I have discussed our intellectual heritage in education, but have said little that is explicit about the art and craft of teaching. The time has come to address these concepts.

Given what I have already said about the kind of science appropriate for education, it should be clear that the space is very large between the ideas that science can provide and the kinds of decisions and actions a teacher must take. Classrooms and students are particular in character. Theory is general. What the teacher must be able to do is see the connection—if there is one—between the principle and the case. But even where such a connection exists, the fit is never perfect.

An imaginative leap is always required. But if we have no rules to follow, then how shall we take this leap? How shall we decide how to act? How do we fill the space between the theoretical frameworks and scientific findings we get from educational research and the concrete realities that we face on the job?

I suggest that it is in this space—the interstices between framework and action—that the art and craft of teaching is most crucial. We face a class, we raise a question, we get little or no response. Theoretical frameworks and the findings of research studies provide only limited help. What we do is to look for clues. We try to read the muted and enigmatic messages in our students' faces, in their posture, in their comportment. We look for a light at one end of the room and then at the other. Our sensibilities come into play as we try to construe the meaning of the particular situation we face.

And what do we face? Do we call on a particular student to get the ball rolling? Do we recast the question? Do we keep on talking and hope for the best? Our educational imagination begins to operate and we consider options. Theory helps, but as a guide not a prescription. It helps us consider options and once selected, we listen for messages given in the tone and pace of our students' conversations and questions. But even these options are options considered in the preactive, rather than in the interactive phase of teaching.

Teaching is typically too dynamic for the teacher to stop in order to formulate hypotheses or to run through a series of theories to form a productive eclectic relationship among them as the basis for deciding on a course of action. Students are not inclined to wait—and teachers know this. Teaching action is more immediate than reflective—unless we have a problem that we cannot solve—and even then reflection is likely to occur outside of the class. The teacher reads the qualitative cues of the situation as it unfolds and thinks on her feet, in many cases like a stand-up comedian. Reflection is not absent, theory is not irrelevant, even research conclusions might be considered, but they provide guidance, not direction. They are more in the background than the forefront of the action.

What we do as teachers is to orchestrate the dialogue moving from one side of the room to the other. We need to give the piccolos a chance—indeed to encourage them to sing more confidently—but we also need to provide space for the brass. And as for the violins, they always seem to have a major part to play. How is it going? What does the melody sound like? Is the music full enough? Do we need to stretch the orchestra further? When shall we pause and recapitulate the intro-ductory theme? The clock is reaching ten and we have not yet crescendoed? How can we bring it to closure when we can't predict when a stunning question or an astute observation will bring forth a new melodic line and off we go again? Such are the pleasures and trials of teaching and when it goes well, there is nothing more that we would rather do.

Is such a story apocryphal? Clearly teachers are not orchestra conduc-tors. Yet teachers orchestrate. The analogue rings true. Is artistry involved? Clearly it is. But where does it occur and of what does it consist? Let me suggest that it occurs first of all in those places—and they are legion—in the conduct of teaching when rules fail.

When rules cannot be used to decode meaning and when prescrip-tions cannot be used to control practice, the teacher must rely on art and craft. To function as an artist or a craftsperson one must be able to read the ineffable yet expressive messages of classroom life. It requires a level of what I have called in previous writings "educational connoisseur-ship"—the ability to appreciate what one has encountered.[20]

But appreciation, even by an educational connoisseur, is not enough. A teacher—like a school administrator—must act. And it is here that another characteristic of the art and craft of teaching comes into play:

The ability to draw on the educational imagination. Like an artist, a teacher must be able to invent moves that will advance the situation from one place in a student's intellectual biography to another. What to do? What kind of question to raise? Do I keep on talking? Do I raise another question? Or do I do something that I never did before? Do I create a new move in another way? Do I let myself fly and thus take the risk of failing? It is here in this pedagogical space that the distinction found in the title of this essay can be explained—"The Art and Craft of Teaching."

What is it that distinguishes the art of teaching from the craft of teaching? It is precisely the willingness and ability to create new forms of teaching—new teaching moves—moves that were not a part of one's existing repertoire.[21] The craftsperson in the classroom has the repertoire, is skilled in its use, and manages the performance quite well indeed. But the craftsperson creates essentially nothing new as a performer. This person's mark is known by the skill with which he or she uses known routines.

The artist in the classroom invents new ones in the process. Such modes of performance are not plentiful, and they require ingenuity and all of the skill that the person possesses. The artist is rarer than the craftsperson. Is the notion of the artist in the classroom really obsolete?

What can we say thus far about what the art and craft of teaching means? First, it means that we recognize that no science of teaching exists, or can exist, that will be so prescriptive as to make teaching routine. The best we can hope for—and it is substantial—is to have better tools from science with which teachers can use their heads.

Second, because the classroom, when not hog-tied or mechanically regimented, is a dynamic enterprise, teachers must be able to read the dynamic structures of signification that occur in such settings. Such reading requires attention to pattern and expressive nuance created by the students and the teacher's own activities.

Third, appreciation is not enough. The teacher must be able to call on or invent a set of moves that create an educationally productive tempo within a class. When we say of some lesson, "It went flat," we mean it both visually and aurally: It had no life, it didn't take hold. What is needed is either, or both, a better reading of the class by the teacher or a more imaginative set of teaching acts.

Fourth, it means that we acknowledge that artistry in teaching represents the apotheosis of educational performance and rather than try to diminish or replace it with rule-governed prescriptions, we ought to offer it a seat of honor. Artistry in teaching is always likely to be rare but it is even rarer when one works in an educational climate that is so concerned about academic achievement that it often stifles intellectual risk-taking on the part of both students and teachers.

This leads me to the final points I wish to address in my examination of the art and craft of teaching. One of those points deals with what it is that we have come to expect from art and craft: the provision of a very special kind of experience we sometimes call aesthetic. Just what does the aesthetic have to do with teaching and education? What is its import? Is it the frosting that makes the cake palatable or is it the marrow of education?

By art in education I am not talking about the visual arts, or music, or dance, but rather about the fact that activities motivated by the aesthetic satisfactions they provide—those that are intrinsic—are among the few that have any durability.[22] Extrinsic rewards for teachers are always likely to be small compared to those secured by people working in other fields. Despite longer vacation periods and sabbaticals, professional opportunities and satisfactions for teachers are limited largely to the lives they lead in their classrooms. Few people regard teachers as receiving handsome salaries—and they are right. The perks related to sabbaticals and vacation periods are distant and short-lived.

When one finds in schools a climate that makes it possible to take pride in one's craft, when one has the permission to pursue what one's educational imagination adumbrates, when one receives from students the kind of glow that says you have touched my life, satisfactions flow that exceed whatever it is that sabbaticals and vacations can provide. The aesthetic in teaching is the experience secured from being able to put your own signature on your own work—to look at it and say it was good. It comes from the contagion of excited students discovering the power of a new idea, the satisfaction of a new skill, or the dilemma of an intellectual paradox that once discovered creates. It means being swept up in the task of making something beautiful—and teachers do make their own spaces and places. They provide, perhaps more than they realize, much of the score their students will experience.

Such moments of aesthetic experience will not of course be constant. We could not, I am convinced, endure it if they were. Only a few scattered throughout the week are enough to keep us going. But without them teaching will be draining rather than nourishing and the likelihood of keeping in teaching those who need and value intellectual stimulation and challenge is very small. The aesthetic moments of teaching are among the deepest and most gratifying aspects of educational life.

But such moments in teaching are not the children of mechanical routine, the offspring of prescriptive rules for teaching, the progeny of rigid lesson plans that stifle spontaneity and discourage exploring the adventitious. Formalized method, bureaucratized procedures, and pressure to get students to perform at any price are their eviscerating conditions. Teachers need the psychological space and the permission to maintain a sense of excitement and discovery for themselves as teachers so that such excitement can be shared with their students.

Does the unabashedly romantic image of teaching I have portrayed have any implications for what we ought to be doing in the schools or is it simply an unrealistic conception of what it means to teach? A conception that will be amply corrected by a Betty Crocker view of teaching or by a teacher-proof curriculum?

I believe the image of the teacher as craftsperson and artist is an ideal toward which we should strive. I believe that our intellectual roots have mistakenly regarded such images as suspect. I believe that many of the solutions being proposed to cure what people believe to be educational ills, solutions such as minimum competency testing, state mandated evaluation procedures, and other legislative panaceas, are fundamentally misguided. They were born of suspicion and tend to motivate by the stick. Human growth and development, whether for teacher or for students, need richer soil in which to flourish. How might such conditions be provided and what might they be? First teachers need to be de-isolated in schools. Hardly anyone knows how or even what their colleagues are doing.

What is the logic in assuming that teachers can be trained once and for all in preservice university programs and then assigned to classrooms for the bulk of their careers with nothing more than brief excursions for inservice education that are usually provided by university professors who themselves have not taught in an elementary or secondary school classroom for a decade or two? The school needs to become a professional community with space enough for teachers to grow as professionals. They have much to offer each other, but these contributions are not easily made when teachers are isolated.

It is well past the time that schools create the organizational structure in which teachers and administrators can reflect on their activities as a regular part of their jobs, not simply within the scope of an inservice education program. Staff development needs to be a continuing part of what it means to be a teacher. The overstaffing of one teacher for every ten would be a step in the right direction. Joint planning could help contribute to it. And a school community that would not judge the quality of its educational program by SAT scores or enrollment in AP courses would also help. Is our educational imagination so impoverished that the only thing we can think of doing for the most able college-bound students is to give them what they will get in college a semester or two later?

We also need administrators who are at least as interested in teaching and curriculum as in organizational maintenance and public relations. We need principals who think of themselves *both* as teachers of teachers and as their teachers' staff. We need school superintendents who can help close the breach between administration and faculty and who remember from whence they came. But how can a principal be an instructional leader when he believes that he knows little about teaching or curriculum?

While it's true that legal mandates, problems between teachers and administrators, and increasingly vocal community concern with the quality of schooling need attention and appropriate professional skills, it is the instructional program and the skill with which it is mediated for which all of the former issues are to be instrumental. Without attention to the instructional program and to the quality of teaching provided, successful arbitration and positive relationships with the community will amount to little from an educational point of view.

At a time when programs in educational administration are focusing on "policy studies" and the "politics of education," it would be ironic if administrators learned how to survive but forgot what survival was for. Our beneficiaries are the students—and without teachers skilled in the craft of teaching, and a curriculum worth teaching, schooling is likely to be educationally vapid.

We need, too, an attitude in schools that expects that experimentation in educational practices is a normal part of doing educational business. Where are the equivalents of Varian's, Xerox's, and IBM's think tanks in our schools? Where are our educational studios? Must we always be in a responsive posture or can we too dream dreams and pursue them?

I said at the beginning of this essay that I was intent on re-establishing the legitimacy of the art and craft of teaching. The image I portrayed at the outset was that of a single individual working painstakingly on something about which he or she cared a great deal. Craftspersons and artists tend to care a great deal about what they do, they get a great deal of satisfaction from the journey as well as from the destination, they take pride in their work, and they are among the first to appreciate quality. Is such an image really inappropriate today? I hope not. I hope such an image always has a place in our schools. And somehow, just somehow, I think that in the private, quiet moments of our professional lives, we do too.

REFERENCES

[1] I am indebted to Ray Bachetti for this tale. Its source is a case study paper that he wrote for Education 279X, Managing in Higher Education, School of Education, Stanford University.

[2] Elwood P. Cubberley, *Public Education in the United States* (Boston: Houghton Mifflin Company, 1934), p. 380.

[3]Ibid., p. 384.

[4]Lawrence Cremin, *The Transformation of the School* (New York: Alfred Knopf, 1961).

[5]Ibid., p. 101.

[6]Ibid., pp. 100–103.

[7]Hall was not only the first editor of *Pedagogical Seminary*, he was its founder. He served as editor from its inception in 1881 to 1924.

[8]William James, *Talks to Teachers on Psychology* (New York: H. Holt & Co., 1901).

[9]Geraldine Joncich, *The Sane Positivist: The Biography of Edward L. Thorndike* (Middletown, Conn.: Wesleyan University Press, 1968).

[10]Ibid., p. 336.

[11]Edward L. Thorndike and Robert S. Woodworth, "The Influences of Special Training on General Ability," *Psychological Abstracts* 7 (March 1900).

[12]Edward L. Thorndike, "The Contribution of Psychology to Education," *Journal of Educational Psychology* 1 (1910): 618.

[13]For a brilliant discussion of this period see, Raymond Callahan, *Education and the Cult of Efficiency* (Chicago: The University of Chicago Press, 1962).

[14]Ibid.

[15]Alfred Jules Ayer, *Language, Truth and Logic* (New York: Dover, no date).

[16]The concept of micro-teaching as the practice of discrete teaching skills is related to this view of the skills of teaching.

[17]The average amount of experimental treatment time for experimental studies reported in the *American Educational Research Journal* in 1977–78 is approximately 45 minutes per subject.

[18]The distinction I wish to underscore is between sciences like anthropology, archeology, and psychoanalysis that aim at explication and those like physics that not only explain but lead to prediction and control.

[19]Because aptitudes for learning different skills and concepts differ among human beings, the effective school will tend to increase individual differences among students rather than diminish them.

[20]Elliot W. Eisner, *The Educational Imagination: On the Design and Evaluation of School Programs* (New York: The Macmillan Company, 1979).

[21]This view of art is based on the work of R. G. Collingwood. See his *Principles of Art* (New York: Oxford University Press, 1958).

[22]Mark Lepper, ed., *The Hidden Cost of Reward* (Hillsdale, N.J.: Erlbaum Associates, 1978).

Chapter 4

These Days—These Debates

Philip L. Hosford

"You can't evaluate me that way. It's too simplistic! There is much more to teaching than just some time-on-task measurement or three visits from my principal who quickly completes the required checklist during each visit."

Mr. Jones was livid and the central office supervisor knew she was getting nowhere with him. Even worse, the debate may continue in different shades of anger, misunderstanding, distrust, and confusion among other teachers and administrators across the land if we fail to translate into practice what we know today about school climate and teacher effectiveness.

Performance evaluation has been mandated in most states and is being implemented one way or another. Performance evaluation systems will vary from state to state and district to district, but the associated debates will all center on the immense complexity of the teaching act, performed by a human being measured as a machine. Over ten years ago I argued that two giant forces were building in education—the first driving toward accountability and the second toward humaneness. Those forces are now center stage in the unfinished plays authored by state legislatures.

THE EITHER-OR ATTITUDE MUST GO

In just the last 30 years we have witnessed many either-or types of national debates in education: phonics vs. sight reading, new math vs. any other kind of math, homogeneous vs. heterogeneous grouping, self-contained classrooms vs. departmentalization, federal aid vs. local control, and behaviorism vs. humanism, to name but a few. History shows that none of these debates was won by either side, but simmered down somewhere in between. In reality few teachers taught reading through just a "phonics" or a "sight-reading" approach. Most teachers used both methods—before, during, and after the great debate of the fifties.

Today, as in the fifties, most teachers use a variety of methods in teaching reading because they are most successful in helping children learn to read when they do so. Similarly, many people never really knew what the new math was other than a few symptomatic elements such as set language. Most would be amazed at how much new math remains in the schools, not because it is new math but because it is valued in teaching and in learning mathematics.

Today, arguments arise between those who advocate the quantitative approach to gaining knowledge about teacher effectiveness and those who advocate the qualitative approach. Once again, history will probably show that both sides have much to offer in resolving the difficult issues. Those who insist on using only one approach delay and obstruct progress and must be helped to see the values offered by using other approaches as well. Specifically, to ignore current teacher effectivenss research is educationally irresponsible. To ignore qualitative aspects of performance evaluation is socially immoral. To ignore them both would indicate rampant dynamic ignorance.

CRITICAL STEPS

If we are to speed the resolution of the performance evaluation problem exemplified by Mr. Jones and his supervisor, we must first recognize the need for both approaches and stop dissipating energies discrediting one another. We must adopt a proactive, problem-solving stance. Second, we must make evaluation of teaching a common, accepted, and valued dimension of instructional improvement. We can all get better; we all want to get better; and we can improve—but only through calm, scholarly evaluations of our teaching for the purpose of self-improvement. Third, we must make it abundantly clear to everyone that summative evaluations for personnel decisionmaking purposes are entirely separate from the formative evaluations used for self-improvement. Only developmental, nonthreatening, formative evaluation procedures will be experienced by 95 percent or more of the staff. The remaining few who have been officially classified as marginal in performance will understand that all evaluation data gathered since the date of such classification can and will be used in a later decision for release, transfer, or reclassification.

IMPROVING TEACHING

Once teacher evaluation for improvement is accepted as standard operating procedure, we must capitalize on the effective teaching research. We must come to understand what research tells us about teacher effectiveness areas such as time-on-task, monitoring, feedback, expectations, success, classroom climate, and management. Consequently, few should fear district-developed methods for gaining time-on-task measurements because the methods would be eminently reasonable, placing the findings in the full context of good education. Concerns about children being on task at worthless activities, or practicing erroneous problem-solving techniques just to be "on task" would vanish because, as professionals, we would all recognize how counterproductive such occupations would be.

Continuously integrated with our understanding and use of the teacher effectiveness research findings would be our awareness of the silent curriculum—which is created only as we teach. This classroom climate and its impact on the affective domain of students and teachers would be part of all evaluations. School _____ conducted by local schools can produce e~~ ᵫable results in this important~~ area. Specifically, districts can and should develop their own menu of strategies for developing a basic desire for learning in all students, improving and bringing closer to reality each student's self-concept, and helping all students gain in their respect for others and for property.

Both a solid knowledge base of teacher effectiveness research and an understanding of the qualitative aspects of teaching are critical to any performance evaluation system. We need both. We must use both. We cannot ignore, or harbor prejudice against, either. Only on this basis can we proceed to develop systems that will resolve the evaluation debate.

PERFORMANCE IMPROVEMENT

Achieving schoolwide consensus regarding the process of performance evaluation is difficult, but now possible. Questions of how and when assessments will be made, by whom, using what measures, and in what way, must all be answered. The criteria for achieving consensus regarding these improvement program questions include the following:

1. Both the science and the art of teaching must be addressed. Any assessment data related to either teacher effectiveness research or the qualitative aspects of teaching must always be placed in the total context of teaching, including class size, facilities, and support services.

2. Assessment processes must be carried out without undue interruption of the instructional program.

3. Procedures and instruments must be developed or approved by faculty and staff.

4. No assessment data will ever be used to threaten.

A school with a data-gathering system meeting these four criteria should rapidly achieve a goal of instructional improvement.

As for Mr. Jones—well, the administration must either (1) give him formal written notice that he is classified as marginal and that from this date forward all data gathered regarding his teaching may be used at a designated date in a summative decision, or (2) stop placing him in a threatening position and help him pursue his own self-development through the established school in-service program.

IN SUMMARY

As professionals, teachers will engage in self-evaluation through school in-service programs and will seek and obtain personal data bases from which to improve if—

1. A clear, unmistakable, legal understanding is reached that, for all those not classified as marginal, all improvement efforts and data gathered are strictly for self-improvement and can never be used to threaten, harass, or coerce.

2. In-service programs provide data and feedback regarding time-on-task, expectations, success rate, and classroom climate, as well as monitoring, feedback, and management skills.

In *Using What We Know About Teaching* (1984 ASCD Yearbook), I suggested several sample methods for measuring various elements of teacher effectiveness and the silent curriculum (climate) that a teacher or faculty might modify, value, and use. Teachers and staff can also develop "measuring procedures" best suited to their own grade level, subject, and population. In any case, feedback on teaching must be available, useful, and helpful. Our desire to improve and become even better teachers than we are can then be realized by incorporating into our staff development programs what is known about both school climate and teacher effectiveness.

Chapter 5

Aldo: A Metaphor

Robert Garmston and Arthur Costa

We have a friend who teaches intermediate grade students. His name is Aldo. He is the father of six and a person of exuberant warmth and great caring for children and animals.

Aldo lives in a farmlike setting where he has surrounded his own children with chickens, pigs, horses, dogs, and cats. Long hours, chores, love, and being together make up this family's life. Each of his children, aged between 10 and 20, has grown into a fine, responsible, loving human being. Two of his children have relatively severe learning disabilities. The eldest, 20, is still dyslexic, still struggles with book learning, yet has saved $10,000 in the bank from part-time jobs and is making plans to start his own business.

Aldo has been a teacher for 25 years. His concern for children is reflected in the long hours he spends in his classroom, before and after school and at noontime. He provides students with a generous amount of individual attention.

Aldo's district has adopted an aggressive staff development program called PRAISED—"Promoting Richer Achievement in Seven Essential Directions." Teachers in the PRAISED program are taught the skills of directed instruction. They are taught four variables of motivation, a five-step lesson plan, six principles of classroom management, and seven ways to deal assertively with discipline problems. Supervisors in the district are taught to supervise and evaluate teaching based on this directed teaching model.

Aldo's principal has several concerns about him. One concern is the jumbled environment of his classroom. Throughout the room numerous student projects appear in various stages of completion. Toothpick sculptures, cardboard dioramas, and maps under construction cover the counter tops and spill onto the floor. Research reports sit in piles and boxes. Students' works of art lend a mosaic/patchwork effect, hanging in proud disarray on cluttered corkboards.

The principal questions Aldo's time on task. For example, periodically Aldo accompanies his class to the public library. The school has no library facility and the public library is approximately 30 minutes away by leisurely stroll. As they amble along, the students interact with each other, often stopping to study and discuss their observations of rocks, birds, insects, and leaves encountered in their path. Aldo's principal is concerned about the loss of instructional time—time that could be spent on mathematics, English, or reading instruction.

Another concern of the principal is that Aldo doesn't turn in his reports on time. His cumulative record entries are sometimes incomplete and seem to lack attention to detail. The principal also believes Aldo is not implementing the PRAISED training.

Word has gone out among the faculty in the district that some teachers may be "praised" and then pushed . . . right out of the district. The word is that someone will be assigned to go into selected classrooms as a followup to the PRAISED training to see how well teachers are doing. It is called coaching. The district is saying this is a way to help teachers. However, there seems to be a strong smell of evaluation in the air.

Aldo is scared. He is literally afraid that, after 25 years of service, he is going to be pushed out. He'd like to comply with whatever it is that is expected of him, but he doesn't quite know if he's capable of doing that.

How can Aldo profit from the resources the district is trying to offer him? Most probably the district's intentions are positive. No one wants to push Aldo out of teaching. On the contrary, the district wants to help. But Aldo would have to change his habits, practices, and perceptions of 25 years. He would have to assume a teaching style and a value system contrary to his own comfortable habits, deep-seated beliefs, and tested strategies for working with children.

Chapter 6

Using Research to Improve Teaching Effectiveness

Ralph W. Tyler

The development and improvement of a profession depends primarily upon the skill and dedication of its practitioners and the relevant knowledge available for their use. This statement appears obvious, but in the teaching profession there is frequently confusion about the knowledge that is relevant and available for teachers to use in the continuing development of their effectiveness.

Knowledge is derived from the interpretation of experience. An individual's experience usually is a series of events that often seem unrelated and unorganized. During every waking minute we are conscious of events that come one after another—an observation of something as we walk, a conversation as we encounter an acquaintance, a discussion with a student, and so on throughout the day. Most educated persons seek to make order out of these unorganized events and to interpret them in a sensible and logical fashion. Knowledge is the result of this effort to understand experience.

Each of us, as teachers, experiences a variety of events relating to our professional responsibility of helping students learn what schools are expected to teach. As we reflect upon our experiences from time to time, we seek to understand them by identifying similarities among several different events and trying to classify these similarities in ways that help us to explain the events and to guide our actions in the future as we encounter situations like those encountered earlier. In this way each of us obtains knowledge from our own experiences. The test of the validity of our interpretation lies in the helpfulness the interpretations provide in our continued professional work. For example, did our interpretation of John's temper tantrum help in our dealing subsequently with his emotional outbursts so that he moved more easily and quickly into constructive activities in the classroom? The knowledge we formulate from personal experience should not be overlooked or belittled in its use in teaching more effectively.

However, we can also gain understanding from the experiences of others, if these experiences are clearly described and the interpretations are properly derived from the data of the events. This is the function of research. Research seeks to gain understanding of a phenomenon usually by identifying factors that help to explain it. Basic research studies in education seek to identify factors that have wide generalizability; that is, they are found to be influential in a wide range of places, situations, teachers, students, and subjects. Inevitably, such generalizations are approximations and do not indicate the variations that may be found in particular situations.

For example, research studies seeking to understand why some inner-city schools are effective in helping children learn what the schools are teaching have found that these schools are staffed by teachers and principals who recognize the importance of the mission of teaching, believe that their students can learn, are perceived by their students as really caring, set standards that are attainable by the students but require considerable effort to reach, and encourage the students to try again when they do not complete a learning task successfully. On the other hand, inner-city schools where little school learning is observed are staffed by teachers and principals many of whom do not believe that their students can learn and who report that they are frustrated and wish to be transferred to a school not in the inner city.

These generalizations were derived from site visits to a number of cities in which the composition of the inner-city neighborhoods varied. Some were composed of recent immigrant families, some of recent arrivals from rural communities, many were composed of members of minority groups. Some of the neighborhoods were centers of crime and vice, but not all. Some were in large public housing complexes, some were in rundown buildings. In this variety of settings, there were variations among both teachers and students. Hence, the particular learning tasks, the particular ways by which teachers communicated their beliefs and attitudes to children were different. And there were differences in the emphases on different learning objectives. Hence, these research studies, as with all basic research investigations, do not provide a what-to-do manual for the improvement of teaching and learning. Research can only report the observations and results of practices actually carried on. It cannot report what would result from a new practice that you or I might invent, although the similarity of our invention to a practice that has been researched should help us to estimate the probable results of our invention.

We must also remember that research findings are generalizations about groups, and do not predict an individual's behavior. This fact is not limited to educational research. For example, physical science research reports the distributions of molecules, atoms, electrons; it does not predict the velocity or other characteristics of an individual molecule, atom, or electron. But this does not mean that we cannot obtain guidance from research in our work with individuals. As we learn about the behavior of groups of students, teachers, parents, and others and obtain estimates of the averages or the factors common to these groups, and their distribution, we have a guide for studying our particular school, classroom, student, teacher, or parent, in order to understand our own situation more fully.

As an example, research studies show that student motivation, clear learning objectives, learning activities that require the student to put forth efforts but are not so difficult that he or she cannot carry them on successfully, satisfaction from success with learning activities, sequential practice, and practice in the use of what is learned in appropriate situations outside the classroom are all influential factors in school learning. The more we understand about such factors, the more complete learning system we, as teachers, have in mind in seeking to understand in our own classes the factors that may not be functioning and those that can be strengthened to improve our instructional efforts. That is, the findings of research furnish a guide for the inquiries, so-called *action research,* that school personnel need to make about the situation in that school. We, as teachers, can use general knowledge helpfully only as we obtain particular knowledge about our programs in promoting and guiding learning, and the problems we encounter. We should not be surprised about this. The best physicians not only keep in touch with relevant medical research but they are also skillful diagnosticians. They collect data about the patient through observation, interview, and the like, and also about the patient's environment. The effective use of medical research requires the physician to carry on his or her own investigations as well.

This emphasis upon the teacher's role in action research raises the question: How do we verify the interpretations of our own inquiries, and the steps we have taken to improve learning? By systematic evaluation of the consequences of the steps we have taken. Has learning improved? The proof of a diagnosis and prescription is in the recovery of the patient. Correspondingly, the proof of our diagnosis of the learning situation and the steps we take to improve it is in the increased learning of the students. Since the teacher is in touch with the students, for many hours over many weeks, he or she has ample opportunity to observe learning and to check the validity of the observations. Hence, systematic evalution does not usually require highly complex or technical evaluation procedures. External testing, in which only 40 minutes or at most 6 hours are available for the tester to obtain evaluation data, requires carefully designed instruments—tests, questionnaires, interview schedules, observation checklists, and the like. Even then, a single test cannot safely be used to make decisions about an individual, because of the possibility of variable factors entering into the situation, where every minute is important. But teachers with their continuing contact with their students can arrive at judgments if the evaluation is carried on as a matter of systematic observation and recording. Errors made in interpretation can be corrected through subsequent observations and data collections.

As examples of the evaluation of improved learning, a teacher can observe the number of students who can now express their communications in clear and orderly sentences; and compare this with the number of an earlier period. The teacher can identify those students who are not successfully carrying on the learning activities. The teacher can check in a variety of meaningful ways the progress students are making toward the learning objective. Those observations can be improved, made more systematic, and the interpretations can be checked by subsequent observations. These evaluation procedures are part of the teaching process, just as the physician expects to check carefully from time to time on the progress of the patient's recovery from illness.

Research gives us guidance—but we, as teachers, are responsible for finding and analyzing our problems, deciding on tentative solutions, testing them, and verifying or refuting our interpretations.

Chapter 7

Overview of Cooperative Learning: A Strategy for Effective Teaching

Chick Moorman, Dee Dishon, and Pat Wilson O'Leary

"Why can't these students get along with each other? Every time I ask them to do group work, there's trouble. They just won't cooperate."

"I've tried groups and they don't work. Students don't get along with each other. Some never get involved. I give up."

These concerns come from teachers we have worked with over the past several years. The teachers care about their students cooperating, getting along, and working together. While their caring remains strong, they don't always know how to remedy the situation. When asked, "How are you teaching cooperation?" most answer, "The students are just supposed to know." These teachers aren't sure what cooperation is, how it is created and maintained, or what skills are necessary to produce it.

Cooperation is a way of behaving that doesn't just happen. It is not something that occurs by accident or by wishing it were there. For cooperation to occur in classrooms, teachers must take an active stance that includes a willingness to structure the environment in a way that invites students to behave cooperatively. Cooperation comes from teachers who purposefully set out to create it by structuring learning tasks in which students practice cooperative skills, learn from their mistakes and successes, and practice again. It comes from teachers who consciously choose to arrange the classroom interaction patterns so that students learn about cooperation. It comes from skilled teachers who deliver skills to students. And it happens on purpose.

The Cooperative Learning model we recommend is one designed by Dee and Pat[1] based on the *Learning Together and Alone* model created by David and Roger Johnson.[2] This skill-oriented method for teaching cooperation is the most successful one we have experienced. By structuring and processing cooperative groups, teachers help students learn about academics, each other, and the social skills necessary to work together productively. In this model, cooperative groups are organized around specific teacher expectations of students and groups and they differ markedly from traditional groups. Let's take a closer look.

STUDENT INTERACTIONS

It is the teacher who determines the interaction patterns of students within the classroom. Teachers decide how students will interact with materials, the teacher, and each other. Of these three patterns, student interaction with each other receives the least amount of attention by teachers. It is also the pattern that holds the most promise for teaching students cooperative skills.

Teachers can choose from three methods of structuring the student–student interactions in their classrooms: competitive, individualistic, and cooperative.

Competitive

When the student–student interactions in a classroom are structured competitively, someone wins and everyone else loses. Examples include spelling bees, reading the most books, rewards for finishing first, and grading on the curve. The outcome in a competitive structure is that if I do well, it hurts your chances of doing well, and if I do poorly, it helps your chances of doing well. The Johnsons state it this way: "If I swim you sink, and if you swim I sink."[2]

Clearly, this structure does little to foster interdependence and cooperation in a classroom. In fact, this structure works against cooperation because it is in the students' self-interest to see that their classmates do poorly.

We are not suggesting that all competition is harmful. If not overdone, it can be energy-producing and motivational. It can also spark interest and be a timely change of pace. Used in abundance, however, competitive student interactions work against creating an "Our Classroom" feeling.[3]

Individualistic

The main characteristic of an individualistic structure is that each student faces the learning situation alone. Examples include each student's having her own workbook page to complete, reading story to finish, art activity to design, or set of math problems to answer.

With an individualistic goal structure, one student's accomplishment does not affect another student's accomplishment, and vice versa. Grades or other rewards are in no way tied to the classroom performance of other students. Each student can earn an A or an E, depending on the individual's accomplishments.

The individualistic structure defines the student–student interaction so that there is no competition and no interdependence. Students are on their own. There is no incentive to work with or against anyone else. As with the competitive structure, constant emphasis on individualistic tasks undermines efforts at creating an "Our Classroom" feeling.

Cooperative

A cooperative structuring of the student–student interaction is an effort to build interdependence. Students are arranged in groups, assigned a single product, and then rewarded on the basis of the group's work on that product. Every group member receives the same reward. If one member does poorly, the whole group is affected. If one member does well, the whole group is also affected.

Examples of single products in cooperatively structured groups include completing one mural, one math paper, or one report, or learning one list of spelling words. Individuals within each group are tied together by the emphasis on a single product as well as a shared reward. These rewards can include extra recess, lining up first, bonus points, or choice time minutes.

Cooperative Learning does *not* mean having students share materials while each individual works on his own workbook page. It does *not* mean having students discuss an assignment together before doing it individually. It does *not* mean having fast finishers help slow finishers. Cooperative Learning as we define and teach it,[1] and as practiced in the Johnsons' model,[2] is much more than students working around a common table, discussing, helping, and sharing materials. Its essence lies in assigning a group goal and then rewarding the group together based on the group product.

RATIONALE FOR TEACHING COOPERATION

Teacher preparation courses have traditionally overlooked the issue of structuring student–student interactions. As a result, teachers have not learned to intentionally create the type of interaction they want between students in their classrooms.

When a teacher is uninformed on the topic of structuring student interactions, the arrangement of learning goals in the classroom is often unclear to both students and teacher. This results in a classroom problem called "fuzzy goal structuring." When the goal is fuzzy, students are unclear as to whether they are competing, working individually, or working cooperatively. When students are unclear about the goal structure, they are unclear about the behaviors that are expected of them. One student showing another how to do a math problem could be viewed as cheating or helping, depending on the goal structure. Likewise, a student not showing another how to do a math problem could be viewed as blocking or helping, depending on the goal structure. Clear goal structures keep students informed as to what behaviors are expected of them.

Also traditionally neglected in teacher preparation courses is the whole issue of cooperation. Teacher training institutions spend little time helping teachers learn how to deliver cooperative skills to students. They place more emphasis on competition and individualization. As a result, many teachers know more about individualization and competition than they do about cooperation. Therefore, most classrooms reflect that imbalance.

CONCERN: Of course there's more emphasis in classrooms on individualization and competition than there is on cooperation. The purpose of education is to prepare students for life. The real world is based on competition. Students need to know how to work well alone and better than everyone else in order to make their mark in our competitive world.

REPLY: What we want to see in classrooms is not the elimination of competitive and individualistic goal structures. We want to see a balance, where cooperation is given the same importance and emphasis as the other two structures. Students need to learn how to work alone so that they can rely on themselves and trust their own judgments and individual abilities. They also need to learn about competition so that they can compete and accept the outcomes of the challenges they choose. Just as important, however, is that students learn how to enter into interdependent relationships, work together for a common goal, and experience the shared joys of successful cooperation. We want students living and learning about competition, individualization, and cooperation now. Education is more than a preparation for life. Education *is* life.

The days of the rugged individualist are gone. Many major contributions to our society no longer come from individuals. Significant contributions come from institutes—from research teams where groups of people work cooperatively to advance science, medicine, technology, and other important areas.

Cooperative skills are necessary for high-quality family living as well. The divorce rate would be affected positively if marriage partners were more skilled in getting along. There would be fewer family crises, fewer runaway adolescents, less child abuse, and more positive, loving relationships if family members had more highly developed cooperative skills.

Cooperation, interdependence, and interpersonal skills that are taught through the use of cooperative groups are appropriate and essential in school, family life, church, community, business, and government. The skills of cooperation and interdependence are essential if we are to survive on a planet of finite and dwindling resources.

DIFFERENCES BETWEEN TYPICAL CLASSROOM GROUPS AND COOPERATIVE GROUPS

The differences between cooperative groups and typical classroom groups are not always apparent to educators untrained in the specifics of cooperative learning. Yet differences exist from preplanning to processing. To help draw a clear distinction between cooperative groups and typical classroom groups, we will examine several issues.

Leadership

Typical classroom groups usually have one leader. That leader, whether chosen by the teacher or the group, is often the best reader, the most popular, or the most assertive group member. Leadership rarely changes although power struggles are frequent.

Leadership in a cooperative group is divided into specific behaviors called social skills. The assumption is that all students can learn these behaviors, so all members are invited to perform and practice them. Leadership is distributed among group members so that everyone leads from time to time. Leadership skills are therefore every group member's responsibility.

Group Makeup

A characteristic of typically organized classroom groups is homogeneity. Reading groups, math groups, and special interest groups tend to clump together students who are most alike. Students don't often have opportunities to work with others of different abilities or interests.

Heterogeneity is the objective of cooperative groups. Such groups are more often dissimilar, with members of each sex, race, interest level, and ability level divided among them.

Success

In typical classroom groups, the success of the individual is unrelated to that of other group members. What one member does has no effect on others. With no interdependence, members have little incentive to cooperate.

In the cooperative group structure, the success of an individual is related to that of all other group members. Because of built-in positive interdependence, students are tied together by shared resources, a group product, or a group reward. The concept "We sink or swim together" is intentionally created.

Resources

In typical classroom groups, each student has all the materials necessary for his own work—textbook, worksheet, pencil, list of spelling words. In cooperative groups, resources are arranged so that (1) there are not enough for everyone (for example, one textbook, one worksheet, one pencil) or (2) each person has a part of the materials that all group members need (for example, two of the ten spelling words, one of the five math problems).

Sharing resources is the strongest way to build the "sink-or-swim-together" feeling in a cooperative group. Without such sharing, group members are more likely to work individually and avoid cooperative behaviors.

Products

In typical classroom groups, group members generally create individual products. Each person turns in her own paper, report, map, or story.

In cooperative groups, the emphasis is on a single product produced by the group. Only one paper, one report, one map, or one story is produced.

Rewards

Rewards in typical classroom groups are passed out individually. Since members turn in individual products, they are rewarded on the basis of those products.

A shared reward is characteristic of cooperative groups. What one group member receives as a reward all group members receive as a reward.

Social Skills

In typical classroom groups, teachers generally tell students to "get along" or "cooperate." Little time is spent on instruction, skill practice, or discussion of what is meant by cooperation. Students are expected to cooperate and often don't have the skills necessary to meet that expectation.

Social skills are an integral part of cooperative groups. They occupy a place of equal importance with subject matter. Time, effort, and attention are given to social skill explanation, practice, feedback, and processing. Teachers believe skilled group members are made, not born, and their actions reflect that belief.

Teachers' Behavior

Teachers who organize typical classroom groups generally behave as *interventionists*. Interventionists believe that students need them to point out when and where they are acting appropriately and inappropriately. These teachers expect to set the standards of effective behavior and believe that they are needed to enforce those behaviors. They rescue individuals and groups.

Teachers who organize cooperative groups generally behave as *interactionists*. Interactionists believe that students learn appropriate and inappropriate behavior by encountering others and being confronted with feedback

47

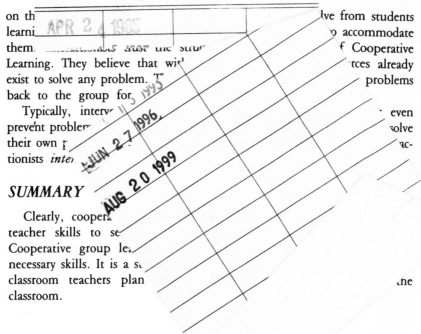
on th_____ lve from students
learni_____ o accommodate
them. _____ f Cooperative
Learning. They believe that wit' ___ rces already
exist to solve any problem. T ___ problems
back to the group for

Typically, interv ___ even
prevent problem ___ solve
their own r ___ ac-
tionists inte

SUMMARY

Clearly, cooper
teacher skills to se
Cooperative group le
necessary skills. It is a s
classroom teachers plan ___ ne
classroom.

REFERENCES

[1]Dishon, Dee, and O'Leary, Pat ____ uidebook for Cooperative Learning: A Technique for Creating Mor. ____ Schools. Holmes Beach, Fla.: Learning Publications, 1984.

[2]Johnson, David, and Johnson, Roger. Learning Together and Alone. Englewood Cliffs, N.J.: Prentice-Hall, 1975.

[3]Moorman, Chick, and Dishon, Dee. Our Classroom: We Can Learn Together. Englewood Cliffs, N.J.: Prentice-Hall, 1983.